TOO MUCH NOISE

Based on an old story from Europe.

Once a woman lived
with her husband
and their children
in a tiny little cottage.
And they had a cat
and a dog as well.

3

All day there was noise.

Her husband sang,
the children played,
the dog barked,
and the cat meowed.

Finally the woman
could stand it no longer.

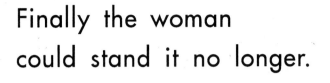

"TOO MUCH NOISE!"
she shouted.
"TOO MUCH NOISE!"
But nobody heard her.

So the woman went
to her wisest friend
and asked her for help.

"I know what to do,"
her friend said.
"Bring your ducks inside."

"What a nonsense!"
thought the woman.
But she brought
the ducks inside
anyway.

The ducks quacked,
her husband sang,
the children played,
the dog barked,
and the cat meowed.

"TOO MUCH NOISE!"
the woman shouted.
"TOO MUCH NOISE!"
But nobody heard her.

10

Again she went to
her wise friend.

"I know what to do,"
said her friend.
"Bring your chickens
inside, too."

"What a nonsense!"
thought the woman.
But she brought
the chickens inside
anyway.

The chickens cackled,
the ducks quacked,
her husband sang,
the children played,
the dog barked,
and the cat meowed.

"TOO MUCH NOISE!"
the woman shouted.
"TOO MUCH NOISE!"
But nobody heard her.

Again she went to
her wise friend.

"I know what to do,"
said her friend.
"Bring your cow inside."

"What a nonsense!"
thought the woman.
But she brought
the cow inside
anyway.

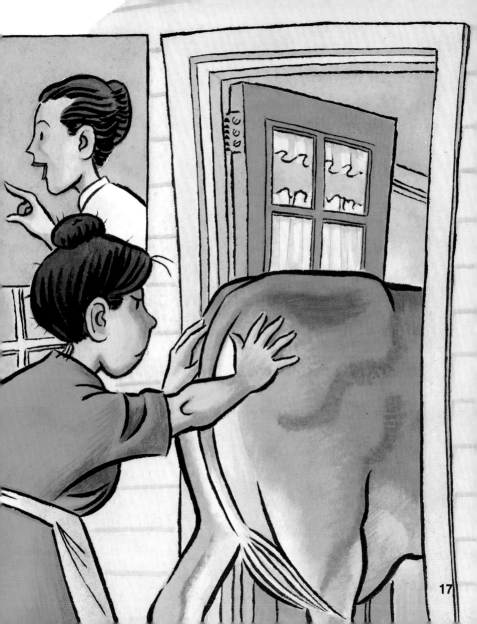

The cow mooed,
the chickens cackled,
the ducks quacked,
her husband sang,
the children played,
the dog barked,
and the cat meowed.

"TOO MUCH NOISE!"
the woman shouted.
"TOO MUCH NOISE!"
But nobody heard her.

Again she went to
her wise friend.

"I know what to do,"
said her friend.
"Take the cow
and the chickens
and the ducks *outside*."

"Take them all *outside*.
What a nonsense!"
thought the woman.
But she took them all
outside anyway.

Out went the cow,
out went the chickens,
and out went the ducks.

Her husband sang,
the children played,
the dog barked,
and the cat meowed.

"Ah," said the woman happily.
"What a nice *quiet* house."